Chapter 1: Understanding AI

What is an AI Influencer?

An AI influencer is a digital persona powered by artificial intelligence, designed to engage, entertain, and inform audiences on social media platforms. Unlike traditional influencers who are humans sharing their personal experiences and opinions, AI influencers are created using advanced algorithms and machine learning techniques. They can simulate human-like interactions, produce content, and even adapt their messaging based on audience feedback. This innovation has opened up a new frontier in social media marketing, allowing brands and individuals to leverage technology for enhanced engagement and reach.

Creating an AI influencer provides an exciting opportunity for anyone looking to enter the social media space. With the right tools and strategies, you can design a virtual personality that resonates with your target audience. This could be a charismatic character with a specific niche focus, such as fashion, travel, or technology. By developing a unique voice and style, your AI influencer can attract followers who are genuinely interested in what it has to say, making it a valuable asset in the crowded social media landscape.

The potential for monetization with an AI influencer is substantial. Once you establish your AI persona and grow its follower base, there are various avenues to generate income. Brands are increasingly interested in partnering with AI influencers for sponsored content, as these digital personas can deliver consistent engagement without the unpredictability that sometimes accompanies human influencers. Additionally, you can explore affiliate marketing, merchandise sales, and exclusive content subscriptions, creating multiple streams of revenue from your AI influencer.

Engagement is key to the success of any influencer, and AI influencers are no exception. By utilizing data analytics, you can monitor audience interactions and preferences, allowing your AI to

1

refine its content strategy continuously. This adaptability is one of the significant advantages AI influencers have over their human counterparts. They can quickly learn from audience feedback, experiment with different types of content, and optimize their approach to maximize engagement and reach.

Building an AI influencer might seem daunting at first, but the process can be incredibly rewarding. With the right mindset, creativity, and willingness to learn, you can create a digital persona that not only entertains but also provides value to its audience. As you embark on this journey, remember that the landscape of social media is ever-evolving, and by embracing the possibilities of AI, you are positioning yourself at the forefront of a revolutionary shift in how influencers are created and monetized.

The Rise of AI in Social Media

The rise of artificial intelligence in social media represents a transformative shift that offers incredible opportunities for aspiring AI influencers. As technology continues to evolve, social media platforms are increasingly integrating AI tools that enhance engagement, personalize content, and streamline interactions. This evolution means that anyone looking to create an AI influencer can harness these powerful tools to not only capture attention but also foster meaningful connections with their audience. Embracing AI in your strategy can elevate your influencer game, enabling you to stand out in a crowded marketplace.

One of the most exciting aspects of AI in social media is its ability to analyze vast amounts of data quickly. This capability allows you to understand your audience's preferences, behaviors, and trends in real time. By leveraging AI analytics, you can tailor your content to resonate with your target demographic, increasing engagement and driving growth. Whether it's identifying the best times to post or the types of content that generate the most interaction, AI equips you with insights that can lead to smarter decisions. This data-driven approach ensures that your efforts are focused and effective, laying a solid foundation for your influencer journey.

Moreover, AI tools can automate many aspects of content creation and scheduling, allowing you to maintain a consistent online presence without the overwhelming time commitment. With advanced algorithms, you can generate visually appealing graphics, engaging videos, and even compelling captions tailored to your audience. This automation not only saves you time but also gives you the freedom to focus on building relationships with your followers. As your AI influencer grows, the ability to efficiently manage your content will be crucial in maintaining momentum and achieving long-term success.

The engagement capabilities of AI also extend to personalized interactions with your audience. Chatbots and AI-driven comment responses can provide immediate engagement, making your followers feel valued and heard. This responsiveness fosters loyalty and encourages community building, which is vital for any influencer. By utilizing AI to enhance your interactions, you can create a more dynamic and engaging platform, ensuring your audience feels a genuine connection to your brand. This personalized approach can significantly contribute to your influencer's reputation and attractiveness for potential partnerships.

Finally, the monetization potential of an AI influencer is vast. With the right strategy and tools in place, you can create an ecosystem that not only attracts followers but also generates revenue. Brands are increasingly looking to collaborate with influencers who can provide unique insights and innovative content, and an AI influencer fits this mold perfectly. By showcasing your ability to leverage technology for creative and engaging content, you'll position yourself as a valuable asset in the social media landscape. The combination of AI and social media is a powerful one, and by embracing it, you are not just building an influencer; you are paving the way for a lucrative and fulfilling career.

Benefits of Using AI Influencers

One of the most significant benefits of using AI influencers is their ability to engage with audiences consistently and effectively. AI influencers can be programmed to interact with followers around the clock, responding to comments, answering questions, and creating a sense of community. This 24/7 availability ensures that your audience feels valued and heard, which can dramatically enhance brand loyalty and engagement. As you build your AI influencer, you'll find that this consistent interaction can lead to a more dynamic presence on social media, helping your brand stand out in a crowded marketplace.

Another advantage of AI influencers is their data-driven approach to content creation. AI technology can analyze vast amounts of data to determine what types of content resonate most with your target audience. By leveraging this information, you can create tailored posts that are more likely to engage and convert your followers. This strategic approach not only saves time but also maximizes your return on investment, making the journey of monetizing your AI influencer more efficient and effective.

Cost efficiency is another key benefit of AI influencers. Unlike traditional influencers, who often require significant financial investments for collaborations, AI influencers can be created and maintained at a fraction of the cost. This affordability allows you to allocate resources to other areas of your business, such as marketing and product development. By utilizing AI influencers, you can achieve a competitive edge without breaking the bank, allowing you to reinvest your savings into further enhancing your social media strategy.

Moreover, AI influencers can operate in various niches and markets, making them incredibly versatile. Whether you're focused on fashion, technology, health, or lifestyle, AI influencers can be tailored to fit your specific needs. This adaptability means you can experiment with different styles and approaches to find what works best for your audience. As you refine your AI influencer, you'll discover the potential to reach diverse demographics and expand your brand's presence across multiple platforms.

Finally, using AI influencers can lead to innovative marketing strategies that human influencers may not be able to replicate. AI influencers can create unique content formats, such as interactive experiences or real-time data visualizations, that engage audiences on a deeper level. This innovation can set you apart from competitors and establish your brand as a forward-thinking leader in your niche. As you embark on your journey to create an AI influencer, embrace the limitless possibilities that come with this technology, and watch your social media presence flourish.

Chapter 2: Defining Your Niche

Identifying Your Target Audience

Identifying your target audience is a crucial step in building your AI influencer. By understanding who your audience is, you can tailor your content and approach to meet their needs and preferences. Start by considering the demographics of your potential followers. Think about age, gender, location, and interests. This information helps you create a clear picture of who you are trying to reach and allows you to craft messages that resonate with them. Remember, the more specific you are, the better you can connect with your audience.

Next, delve into the psychographics of your target audience. This involves understanding their values, attitudes, lifestyles, and behaviors. What motivates them? What are their pain points? By answering these questions, you can create content that not only entertains but also provides solutions to their problems. Engaging with your audience on a deeper emotional level will build trust and loyalty, making them more likely to follow and engage with your AI influencer.

Utilizing social media analytics tools can significantly enhance your understanding of your target audience. These tools provide insights into who is engaging with your content, their interests, and how they interact with your posts. By analyzing these metrics, you can refine your approach, adapting your content strategy to better align with your audience's preferences. Don't shy away from experimenting with different types of content to see what resonates most. The key is to stay flexible and responsive to the feedback you receive.

In addition to analytics, consider conducting surveys or polls to gather direct feedback from your audience. This not only shows that you value their opinions but also provides you with valuable insights into what they want to see more of. Engaging with your audience in this way can create a sense of community and belonging, further solidifying their connection to your AI influencer. Remember, your audience's needs may evolve over time, so staying in tune with their preferences is essential for long-term success.

As you refine your understanding of your target audience, you will find that your content becomes more focused and impactful. This clarity will not only enhance your engagement rates but also open doors for monetization opportunities. Brands and businesses are keen to collaborate with influencers who have a clear understanding of their audience, as it ensures that their products are reaching the right people. By investing the time and effort into identifying your target audience, you are setting the stage for a successful AI influencer career that can generate income and foster meaningful connections.

Analyzing Market Trends

Analyzing market trends is a crucial step in building your AI influencer and finding success on social media. Understanding current trends allows you to align your content with what audiences are actively engaging with, ensuring that your AI influencer remains relevant and appealing. Start by researching popular topics within your niche, utilizing tools like Google Trends, social media analytics, and industry reports. By identifying patterns in user behavior, you can craft content that resonates with your target audience, ultimately driving engagement and growth.

In addition to identifying trends, it's essential to analyze your competitors' strategies. Take note of the successful AI influencers in your field and dissect their content, engagement tactics, and audience interactions. This analysis will provide invaluable insights into what works and what doesn't. Look for gaps in their content that you can fill, or innovative ideas that you can adapt to suit your unique style. By learning from others, you can create a distinctive brand identity that sets your AI influencer apart in a crowded marketplace.

Don't overlook the importance of audience feedback in your trend analysis. Engaging with your audience through polls, comments, and direct messages can yield critical information about their preferences and expectations. Use this feedback to refine your content strategy, ensuring that you address the interests and concerns of your followers. By fostering a two-way communication channel, you not only build a loyal community but also empower your AI influencer to evolve with the changing dynamics of social media.

As you continue to analyze market trends, remember to stay adaptable. Social media is a fast-paced environment, and what is trending today may change tomorrow. Regularly revisit your analysis to stay ahead of the curve. Embrace new platforms, explore emerging technologies, and pay attention to shifts in user behavior. Being proactive rather than reactive will position your AI influencer for long-term success, allowing you to capitalize on new opportunities as they arise.

Finally, leverage data to inform your decisions. Utilize analytics tools to track the performance of your content and measure audience engagement. This quantitative data will help you refine your strategies and make informed decisions about future content. By establishing a data-driven approach, you can enhance your AI influencer's effectiveness and maximize its potential for monetization. With diligence and creativity, you can turn your analysis into actionable insights, paving the way for a thriving AI influencer that not only captivates audiences but also generates revenue on social media.

Choosing Your Unique Selling Proposition

Choosing your unique selling proposition (USP) is a crucial step in establishing your AI influencer. Your USP is what sets you apart from the competition and defines the value you offer to your audience. Given the rapidly expanding landscape of social media, it's essential to articulate what makes your AI influencer distinct. Take the time to reflect on your core strengths, values, and interests.

Consider what niche your AI influencer will occupy and how it aligns with current trends. This foundation will not only guide your content creation but also appeal to a specific audience eager for unique insights and perspectives.

To effectively identify your USP, begin by conducting thorough research on existing influencers in your chosen niche. Analyze their content, engagement strategies, and audience interactions. Look for gaps or areas that are underserved, and think about how your AI influencer can fill those spaces. This research phase is vital as it helps you understand what resonates with audiences and what doesn't. By recognizing these opportunities, you can craft a USP that not only distinguishes your influencer but also addresses the needs and desires of your target audience.

Once you have a clear understanding of your niche and the competitive landscape, it's time to develop your unique message. This message should encapsulate your influencer's personality, expertise, and the value it provides. Whether your AI influencer is informative, entertaining, or a blend of both, ensure that this message is consistent across all platforms. Consistency builds trust, and trust is essential for converting followers into loyal fans. As you craft your message, think about the tone and style that will best resonate with your audience. This is your opportunity to showcase your AI influencer's voice and engage with followers on a personal level.

Incorporating storytelling into your USP can significantly enhance its appeal. People connect with narratives, so think about the stories you want your AI influencer to tell. These can be personal anecdotes, lessons learned, or even fictional tales that align with your influencer's persona. Stories can make your content relatable and memorable, fostering a deeper connection with your audience. When your followers feel a connection, they are more likely to engage, share, and support your content, ultimately driving the success of your AI influencer.

Finally, don't hesitate to refine your USP as you grow. The digital landscape is always evolving, and your AI influencer should adapt to changes in audience preferences and market trends. Regularly seek feedback from your audience and monitor engagement metrics to gauge the effectiveness of your USP. Embrace the iterative process of growth and improvement. By being open to change and continuously honing your unique selling proposition, you can ensure that your AI influencer remains relevant, engaging, and profitable in the ever-competitive world of social media.

Chapter 3: Selecting the Right AI Tools

Overview of AI Influencer Platforms

AI influencer platforms are revolutionizing the way individuals and brands interact with social media. These platforms leverage artificial intelligence to create virtual influencers that can engage audiences, promote products, and even create original content. This innovation allows anyone to step into the world of influencing without the traditional barriers faced by human influencers, such as time constraints, personal branding challenges, or the need for a large following. The potential to monetize an AI influencer is vast, offering unique opportunities for creativity and financial gain.

At the heart of AI influencer platforms is the ability to customize your virtual persona. Users can design their AI influencers with specific traits, appearances, and backstories that resonate with their target audience. This personalization ensures that the AI influencer aligns perfectly with niche markets, whether it's fashion, gaming, health, or technology. By tapping into these niches, you can attract a dedicated fan base, making it easier to monetize through sponsorships, merchandise, or affiliate marketing. The flexibility of these platforms empowers you to create an influencer that truly reflects your vision.

Another significant advantage of using AI influencer platforms is the data-driven insights they provide. These platforms often come equipped with analytics tools that allow you to track engagement, reach, and audience demographics. By understanding what works and what doesn't, you can refine your content strategy to maximize your impact. This analytical approach not only helps in growing your audience but also in making informed decisions about collaborations and marketing strategies, paving the way for sustainable income streams.

Moreover, the scalability of AI influencers is unmatched. Unlike human influencers who may have limitations due to time or availability, AI influencers can operate around the clock. They can engage with followers in real-time, respond to comments, and even post content consistently without the fatigue that comes with traditional influencer work. This continuous presence enhances brand visibility and keeps your audience engaged, thereby increasing your chances of monetization through various avenues, such as sponsored posts, brand partnerships, and product launches.

Finally, the community surrounding AI influencer platforms is growing rapidly, providing a wealth of resources and support for aspiring creators. From forums and online courses to social media groups, you can find guidance and inspiration from others who are on the same journey. This collaborative environment encourages innovation and experimentation, allowing you to learn from others' successes and challenges. By embracing this supportive network, you'll be well-equipped to build a successful AI influencer that not only resonates with your audience but also generates income and fulfills your creative aspirations.

Key Features to Look For

When embarking on the journey to create an AI influencer, understanding the key features that will set your digital persona apart is crucial. First and foremost, consider the personality traits of your AI influencer. A relatable and engaging personality can draw in followers and create a loyal fan base. Think about the tone of voice, humor, and values your AI will embody. Aligning these traits with your target audience's interests will foster a deeper connection, making your influencer more appealing and marketable.

Next, focus on the visual aesthetics of your AI influencer. The avatar's design should be eye-catching and reflective of the niche you are targeting. Whether it's a sleek, modern look or a more whimsical appearance, consistency in visual branding will help your influencer stand out in a crowded social media landscape. High-quality graphics and animations can elevate the overall appearance and professionalism of your content, making it more likely to attract and retain followers.

In addition to personality and aesthetics, the functionality of your AI influencer is vital. Consider incorporating advanced features such as interactive engagement capabilities, where followers can ask questions or participate in polls. This interaction will not only enhance user experience but also provide valuable insights into your audience's preferences. The more engaging and responsive your AI is, the more likely it is to build a community and drive monetization opportunities through sponsorships and collaborations.

Moreover, ensure that your AI influencer is adaptable and capable of evolving with trends. Social media is a rapidly changing environment, and your influencer must stay relevant. This means regularly updating content strategies and being responsive to audience feedback. Implementing machine learning algorithms can help your AI learn from interactions and optimize its content, ensuring it remains fresh and appealing to followers over time.

Finally, consider the monetization strategies that will maximize your AI influencer's potential. From affiliate marketing to brand partnerships, understanding how to effectively monetize your content will be key to turning your venture into a profitable endeavor. Explore various revenue streams, including merchandise sales and exclusive content subscriptions. By focusing on these key features, you can create a compelling AI influencer that not only captivates audiences but also generates income, paving the way for long-term success in the social media landscape.

Comparison of Popular Tools

When embarking on the journey to create your AI influencer, understanding the tools at your disposal is crucial for success. Each tool offers unique features that cater to different aspects of influencer creation and management. By comparing popular tools, you can make informed decisions that will streamline your process and enhance your social media presence. This comparison will empower you to choose the best tools that align with your vision and goals, ultimately leading to a profitable venture.

One of the leading tools in AI content generation is OpenAI's GPT-3. This platform allows you to create engaging and relatable content tailored to your audience's interests. With its advanced language model, you can generate posts, captions, and even responses to comments that resonate with your followers. Additionally, its versatility means you can adapt the tone and style to fit the persona of your AI influencer. The ability to produce high-quality content quickly will save you time and effort, enabling you to focus on growing your brand.

For visuals, tools like Canva and Daz 3D are invaluable. Canva offers an intuitive interface for designing eye-catching graphics, while Daz 3D allows you to create stunning 3D avatars that can serve as the face of your AI influencer. Both tools empower creators to produce professional-looking visuals without requiring extensive design skills. By leveraging these platforms, you can ensure that your social media posts are not only engaging but also visually appealing, which is essential for capturing attention in a crowded digital landscape.

Social media management tools such as Hootsuite and Buffer play a significant role in maintaining a consistent online presence. These platforms enable you to schedule posts, analyze performance metrics, and engage with your audience from a single dashboard. By utilizing these tools, you can streamline your workflow and ensure that your content reaches your followers at optimal times. Consistency is key to building a loyal audience, and effective management will help you achieve that while freeing up time for other creative endeavors.

Lastly, analytics tools like Sprout Social and Google Analytics provide insights into how your content is performing. Understanding metrics such as engagement rates, audience demographics, and peak activity times will help you refine your strategy. By analyzing this data, you can make informed decisions about what content resonates most with your audience, allowing you to tailor your approach for maximum impact. Embracing these tools will not only enhance your understanding of your audience but also pave the way for monetization opportunities as you grow your AI influencer brand.

Chapter 4: Creating Your AI Influencer's Personality

Defining Your Influencer's Voice

Defining your influencer's voice is a critical step in the journey of creating a successful AI influencer. This voice will serve as the foundation for all interactions, content, and engagements across social media platforms. It's essential to ensure that the voice resonates with your target audience while reflecting the personality and values of your AI influencer. Take the time to brainstorm the characteristics you want your influencer to embody. Should they be witty and humorous or more serious and informative? This will help you establish a consistent tone that attracts and retains followers.

Once you have a clear idea of your influencer's personality, you can begin to craft their unique voice. Think about the language they would use, their style of communication, and how they would respond to various situations. For example, an AI influencer that appeals to a young, trendy demographic might use casual language and current slang, while one aimed at professionals might adopt a more polished and formal tone. By defining these elements, you set the stage for authentic interactions that will engage your audience and encourage them to follow and trust your influencer.

Consider the type of content your AI influencer will produce. Whether it's informative blog posts, entertaining videos, or engaging social media updates, the voice must remain consistent across all formats. This consistency helps build brand recognition and fosters a loyal community. You can also create a guideline document that outlines key phrases, preferred language, and tone variations for different scenarios, ensuring that your influencer's voice remains cohesive no matter the platform or context.

Testing and refining your influencer's voice is an ongoing process. Pay attention to audience reactions and engagement metrics, as they will provide valuable insights into what resonates with your followers. Don't hesitate to experiment with different styles and tones to see how they impact engagement. If your audience responds positively to a particular approach, lean into it and make it a staple of your influencer's voice. This adaptability will not only enhance the authenticity of your influencer but also keep the content fresh and exciting.

Ultimately, defining your AI influencer's voice is about creating a relatable persona that can connect with followers on a personal level. By carefully curating this voice, you can cultivate a community that feels engaged and invested in your influencer's journey. Remember, the goal is to create an influencer that not only shares valuable content but also fosters a sense of belonging and interaction among followers. With a strong, defined voice, your AI influencer is well on its way to becoming a trusted figure in the social media landscape, paving the path for monetization and success.

Building a Compelling Backstory

Building a compelling backstory is essential for creating an AI influencer that resonates with your audience. Your AI's history can shape its personality, values, and the way it interacts with followers. To establish a strong foundation, consider the characteristics you want your AI influencer to embody. Is it relatable, aspirational, or perhaps a combination of both? Think about how these traits can reflect the journey and experiences that make your AI unique. A well-crafted backstory not only engages followers but also builds trust and loyalty, which are crucial for monetization.

When developing your AI influencer's backstory, start by outlining its origins. Where did it come from, and what inspired its creation? This could be a narrative about the technology that powers it or a fictional tale that gives it a relatable context. For instance, your AI might be designed to promote sustainability, stemming from a fictional backstory of witnessing environmental challenges. This narrative can serve as a powerful tool to connect with an audience that shares similar values, making your AI influencer more appealing and credible.

Next, delve into the AI's key experiences and milestones. Just like any human influencer, your AI should have a journey filled with challenges, triumphs, and learning moments. These experiences can be shared through engaging content, such as stories or posts that highlight specific milestones in your AI's development. By showcasing these moments, you not only humanize your AI but also create opportunities for followers to engage with its story. This engagement can lead to increased visibility and, ultimately, more opportunities for monetization.

Another crucial aspect of your AI influencer's backstory is its relationships and community. Establishing connections with other influencers, brands, or even fictional characters can enhance your AI's credibility. Think about how your AI interacts with its environment and followers. Building a network through collaborations or supportive interactions can create a sense of community, encouraging followers to become advocates for your AI. This sense of belonging can significantly boost your AI's popularity and, consequently, its monetization potential.

Finally, remember to keep your AI's backstory dynamic. As your AI influencer grows and evolves, so should its narrative. Regularly updating followers with new developments or changes in its story keeps the content fresh and engaging. Encourage interaction by inviting followers to contribute ideas or share their experiences related to your AI's journey. This not only deepens the connection but also keeps your audience invested in your AI influencer's success, ultimately paving the way for monetization opportunities that can turn your vision into reality.

Crafting Engaging Content Styles

Creating engaging content styles is essential for any AI influencer looking to make a mark on social media. The digital landscape is

crowded, and standing out requires more than just quality; it demands creativity and authenticity. Begin by identifying your target audience and understanding their preferences. This foundational knowledge allows you to tailor your content style to resonate with them. Whether your audience prefers humor, inspiration, or educational content, aligning your style with their interests will significantly enhance engagement.

Once you have a grasp of your audience, experiment with different content formats. Videos, infographics, memes, and blog posts each offer unique opportunities to connect. For instance, short, snappy videos can capture attention quickly, while detailed blog posts can establish you as an authority in your niche. Mixing formats keeps your content fresh and exciting, encouraging your followers to interact and share. Remember, the goal is to create a diverse content palette that caters to various preferences while remaining true to your brand.

Storytelling is a powerful technique that can elevate your content style. People are naturally drawn to stories, and using them in your posts can create emotional connections with your audience. Share personal experiences, successes, and challenges faced on your journey to becoming an AI influencer. By opening up and being relatable, you invite your audience into your world, making them more likely to engage with your content. This approach not only boosts interaction but also fosters a loyal community around your brand.

Visual elements play a crucial role in crafting engaging content. High-quality images, graphics, and videos are essential to capturing attention amidst the noise of social media. Invest time in creating visually appealing posts that reflect your unique style. Consistency in color schemes, fonts, and overall aesthetics helps establish brand identity and makes your content instantly recognizable. Pairing strong visuals with compelling captions can significantly enhance engagement and encourage followers to share your content with their networks.

Finally, don't shy away from seeking feedback and adapting your content style based on what resonates most with your audience. Monitor engagement metrics, read comments, and utilize polls to understand what your followers love. This willingness to evolve not only keeps your content relevant but also shows your audience that you value their input. As you refine your content strategies, you'll find your AI influencer brand becoming more engaging and profitable, paving the way for success in the dynamic world of social media.

Chapter 5: Designing Your AI Influencer

Choosing an Aesthetic

Choosing an aesthetic for your AI influencer is a crucial step that can profoundly impact your brand identity and audience engagement. Your aesthetic is not just about visual appeal; it encompasses the overall vibe and message you want to convey. Consider the emotions you want to evoke in your audience and how you wish to be perceived in your niche. Whether your AI influencer will embody a sleek, modern look or a whimsical, playful vibe, defining this aesthetic will help streamline your content creation and marketing strategies.

Once you have a clear vision of your aesthetic, it's time to explore color palettes, fonts, and imagery that resonate with your theme. Colors evoke feelings, so select a palette that reflects the personality of your AI influencer. For instance, vibrant colors may suggest energy and creativity, while muted tones could convey sophistication and calm. Consistency in your visual elements will create a recognizable brand, allowing your audience to identify your content instantly, which is vital in the crowded social media landscape.

Next, think about the style of content that aligns with your chosen aesthetic. Will your AI influencer share lifestyle tips, fashion inspiration, or motivational quotes? Each type of content can be tailored to fit your aesthetic, but it's essential to maintain a cohesive approach. If your aesthetic is minimalistic, for example, your posts should feature clean lines and straightforward messaging. By curating your content to reflect your aesthetic, you will build a strong connection with your audience, encouraging them to engage and share your posts.

Engagement is key to monetizing your AI influencer. As you develop your aesthetic, consider how it can facilitate interactions with your audience. Use polls, questions, and calls to action that align with your aesthetic to spark conversations. The more you engage with your followers, the more invested they will become in your journey. This engagement not only strengthens your community but also enhances your potential for partnerships and sponsorships, ultimately leading to monetary success.

Lastly, remember that your aesthetic can evolve over time. As trends shift and your audience grows, don't hesitate to refine your aesthetic to keep it fresh and relevant. Stay attuned to feedback from your followers and the broader social media landscape. By remaining adaptable while staying true to your core values, you can ensure that your AI influencer remains appealing and profitable in the long run. Embrace the process of choosing your aesthetic, as it's a powerful tool in building a successful AI influencer that resonates with audiences and drives revenue.

Creating Visual Content

Creating visual content is a pivotal step in establishing your AI influencer and capturing the audience's attention. The world of social media is inherently visual, with platforms like Instagram, TikTok, and YouTube thriving on stunning imagery and engaging videos. To stand out, you must develop a unique visual style that resonates with your target audience. Start by defining your brand's aesthetic. Consider the colors, fonts, and overall vibe that will represent your AI influencer. This consistency will help in building a recognizable identity that followers can connect with, fostering trust and loyalty.

Next, invest time in learning the basics of graphic design and video editing. Numerous online tools and resources can assist you in creating high-quality visuals without requiring extensive technical skills. Platforms like Canva and Adobe Spark offer user-friendly templates that can help you produce eye-catching graphics. For video content, apps like InShot and Adobe Premiere Rush allow you to edit videos on your smartphone efficiently. By mastering these tools, you can create professional-looking content that reflects the personality of your AI influencer and engages your audience effectively.

Incorporating user-generated content into your strategy can further enhance your visual presence. Encourage your followers to share their experiences with your AI influencer and tag your account. This not only provides you with authentic content to share but also fosters a sense of community among your audience. Showcasing your followers' content demonstrates appreciation and builds a stronger connection, making your influencer more relatable and appealing. Remember, the more your audience feels involved, the more likely they will share your content and expand your reach.

Don't underestimate the power of storytelling through visuals. Every image or video you create should convey a message or evoke emotions that align with your brand. Use captions, graphics, and visuals that tell a story, whether it's about overcoming challenges or celebrating successes. Storytelling can captivate your audience and make your AI influencer memorable. When followers feel emotionally connected to your content, they are more likely to engage with it, share it, and even convert into loyal customers.

Finally, consistently analyze the performance of your visual content. Use analytics tools available on social media platforms to understand what resonates with your audience. Look for patterns in engagement, such as likes, comments, and shares. This data will inform your future content creation, allowing you to refine your strategies and focus on what works best. By staying adaptable and responsive to your audience's preferences, you will not only enhance your AI influencer's visual appeal but also increase your chances of monetizing your presence on social media. Embrace this journey, and watch your AI influencer thrive!

Utilizing AI for Design

In the rapidly evolving landscape of social media, utilizing AI for design can propel your AI influencer from concept to reality with remarkable efficiency. The beauty of AI design tools lies in their ability to streamline the creative process, allowing you to focus on building your brand and engaging with your audience. By leveraging platforms that harness artificial intelligence, you can generate stunning visuals, create engaging content, and maintain a consistent aesthetic that captivates your followers. This not only saves time but also enhances the overall quality of your influencer's presence online.

One of the most powerful applications of AI in design is the ability to create personalized graphics and videos tailored to your audience's preferences. AI algorithms can analyze user engagement data to determine which styles, colors, and themes resonate most with your followers. By using AI-powered design tools, you can quickly produce eye-catching posts that align with your audience's interests. This targeted approach ensures that your content stands out in a crowded social media landscape, increasing the likelihood of shares and interactions that can boost your visibility.

Moreover, AI can assist in automating repetitive design tasks, freeing up your creative energy for more innovative projects. You can set up templates for your posts, stories, and promotional materials, allowing the AI to adapt these templates based on real-time trends and audience feedback. This adaptability not only keeps your content fresh and relevant but also allows you to maintain a consistent posting schedule, which is crucial for growing your follower base. Consistency helps establish your AI influencer as a reliable source of content, encouraging followers to engage and share your work.

Incorporating AI-generated insights into your design process can also enhance your overall strategy. By analyzing what types of visual content perform best, AI tools can guide you in fine-tuning your design choices. These insights can inform your decisions about color schemes, font styles, and layout designs that encourage higher engagement. Understanding your audience's preferences through data-driven insights allows you to create designs that not only look good but also perform well in terms of reach and interaction.

Finally, the integration of AI into your design workflow can open up new revenue streams for your AI influencer. As your follower count grows, you can leverage your unique aesthetic and the data collected from your audience to collaborate with brands or even launch your own products. By showcasing your ability to create captivating designs consistently, you position your AI influencer as a valuable asset in the eyes of potential partners. With the right approach, the skills you develop in utilizing AI for design can lead to monetization opportunities that transform your passion for social media into a profitable venture.

Chapter 6: Developing a Content Strategy

Planning Your Content Calendar

Planning your content calendar is a crucial step in building your AI influencer and ensuring your social media success. A well-structured calendar helps you stay organized, maintain consistency, and engage your audience effectively. Start by defining your goals and what you want to achieve with your content. Consider the message you want to convey and how it aligns with your brand identity. With clear objectives, you can tailor your content to resonate with your audience and drive engagement.

Next, identify the key themes and topics that will form the backbone of your content strategy. These themes should reflect your niche and the interests of your target audience. Conduct research to understand trending topics, popular hashtags, and the kind of content that resonates with your followers. By focusing on relevant themes, you can create content that not only attracts attention but also establishes your authority in the niche of AI influencers.

Once you have your themes in place, it's time to create a posting schedule. Decide how often you want to post and the best times to reach your audience. Consistency is vital, so aim for a regular posting rhythm that keeps your followers engaged. You might choose to post daily, several times a week, or weekly, depending on your resources and the preferences of your audience. Utilize tools like scheduling software to streamline the process and ensure your content is shared at optimal times.

Incorporate a mix of content types into your calendar to keep things fresh and engaging. This could include images, videos, stories, polls, and live sessions. Mixing formats not only increases engagement but also allows you to showcase the versatility of your AI influencer. Balance promotional content with value-driven posts that educate or entertain your audience. This strategy fosters trust and builds a loyal follower base that supports your monetization efforts.

Finally, regularly review and adjust your content calendar based on performance metrics and audience feedback. Monitor engagement rates, reach, and other analytics to understand what works and what doesn't. Be flexible and willing to pivot your strategy as needed. By staying attuned to your audience's preferences and adapting your content accordingly, you will maximize your potential to monetize your AI influencer and achieve your social media goals. Embrace the journey, and remember that each step you take brings you closer to success.

Types of Content to Produce

When embarking on the journey to build your AI influencer, understanding the types of content you can produce is crucial for standing out in the crowded social media landscape. Engaging visuals are at the forefront of effective content creation. High-quality images, eye-catching graphics, and compelling animations can captivate your audience's attention, making them more likely to share and interact with your posts. By leveraging tools that allow your AI influencer to generate stunning visuals, you can create a unique aesthetic that reflects your brand and resonates with your target audience.

Video content is another powerful medium that can elevate your AI influencer's presence. Short clips, tutorials, and live streams can establish a deeper connection with your followers, fostering a sense of community and engagement. Consider creating behind-the-scenes videos that showcase the personality and creativity of your AI influencer. This not only humanizes your brand but also encourages viewers to invest emotionally in your content. With platforms favoring video, it's an opportunity you shouldn't overlook.

User-generated content is a fantastic way to build credibility and trust. By encouraging your audience to share their own experiences related to your niche, you can create a wealth of content while fostering a strong sense of community. Consider running contests or challenges that inspire your followers to contribute their own content, which you can then share on your platforms. This not only showcases your audience's creativity but also reinforces their connection to your AI influencer, leading to increased loyalty and brand advocacy.

Educational content is invaluable in positioning your AI influencer as an authority in your niche. Create informative blog posts, infographics, and how-to videos that provide real value to your audience. Sharing your expertise not only helps to grow your following but also encourages your audience to return for more insights. This strategy can be particularly effective in niches where people are eager to learn, as it establishes your influencer as a go-to resource for knowledge and guidance.

Finally, don't underestimate the power of storytelling. Craft narratives that resonate with your audience, whether through inspirational posts, personal anecdotes, or fictional tales featuring your AI influencer. Storytelling can evoke emotions and create a lasting impression, making your content more memorable. By weaving your influencer's journey into your posts, you can inspire and motivate your audience, turning casual followers into dedicated fans who are eager to support your monetization efforts on social media.

Engaging with Your Audience

Engaging with your audience is a crucial step in establishing your AI influencer in the competitive social media landscape. When you create content that resonates with your followers, you build a community that not only appreciates your work but also actively participates in your journey. Start by understanding your audience's preferences and interests. Use tools and analytics to gather insights about their demographics, engagement patterns, and feedback. This knowledge will empower you to tailor your messages, ensuring they strike a chord with your viewers and foster a sense of belonging.

One effective way to engage your audience is through interactive content. Polls, quizzes, and Q&A sessions invite your followers to share their thoughts, making them feel valued and included. These interactions can spark discussions that enhance your relationship with your audience. Additionally, consider hosting live sessions where you can address questions in real time, share behind-the-scenes glimpses of your AI influencer creation process, or even showcase your AI's unique capabilities. Such transparency not only builds trust but also enhances the excitement around your brand.

Storytelling is another powerful tool for engagement. People connect with stories on a personal level, so weaving narratives into your content can significantly elevate your influence. Share your journey, the challenges you faced while building your AI influencer, and the successes you achieved along the way. Your audience will appreciate your authenticity and may see reflections of their own aspirations in your story. This emotional connection can transform passive followers into active supporters who are eager to share your content and spread your message.

Consistency is key in maintaining engagement over time. Develop a content calendar that outlines your posting schedule, ensuring that you're consistently sharing valuable and entertaining material. This regularity helps keep your audience engaged, as they come to anticipate your posts and look forward to each new piece of content. Additionally, make it a point to respond to comments and messages promptly. Acknowledging your followers' input demonstrates that you care about their opinions, fostering a loyal community that feels invested in your growth.

Finally, leverage collaborations to broaden your reach and engage with new audiences. Partnering with other influencers or brands can introduce your AI influencer to different demographics, creating fresh opportunities for interaction. Choose collaborators who align with your values and vision to ensure that the partnership feels authentic. By combining forces, you not only expand your audience but also create diverse content that can capture the interest of both sets of followers. Embrace these strategies to engage with your audience effectively, and watch as your AI influencer flourishes in the dynamic world of social media.

Chapter 7: Setting Up Social Media Profiles

Choosing the Right Platforms

Choosing the right platforms for your AI influencer is a crucial step in ensuring your success on social media. Each platform has its unique audience, features, and content styles, which can significantly impact how your AI influencer is perceived and how effectively it engages with followers. Understanding these nuances will empower you to select the platforms that align best with your goals, allowing you to maximize your reach and monetization potential.

Start by identifying where your target audience spends their time online. For instance, younger demographics tend to gravitate towards platforms like TikTok and Instagram, where visual content reigns supreme. Alternatively, if your AI influencer caters to professionals or a more mature audience, LinkedIn might be the ideal choice. Researching demographics and platform usage will provide valuable insights, guiding you toward the most promising avenues for engagement and growth.

Once you have pinpointed potential platforms, consider the type of content your AI influencer will create. Some platforms thrive on short, engaging videos, while others may favor long-form articles or eye-catching images. Tailor your content strategy to fit the strengths of each platform. For example, if you choose Instagram, focus on high-quality visuals and stories that captivate viewers. If TikTok is your choice, think about creative, entertaining videos that resonate with trends. This alignment will enhance your influencer's appeal and increase the chances of going viral.

As you select your platforms, don't forget about the importance of cross-promotion. Creating a cohesive brand presence across multiple platforms can amplify your reach and reinforce your message. For instance, you can use TikTok to drive followers to your Instagram account, where you might share more in-depth content or exclusive offers. This interconnected strategy not only increases visibility but also fosters a loyal community around your AI influencer, enhancing engagement and driving monetization opportunities.

Finally, keep in mind that the digital landscape is always evolving. Stay informed about emerging platforms and trends that could provide new opportunities for your AI influencer. Don't hesitate to experiment with different channels to see what resonates best with your audience. By remaining adaptable and open to change, you can position your AI influencer for continued growth and success in the dynamic world of social media. Embrace the journey, and remember that the right platforms can be the key to unlocking your influencer's full potential.

Optimizing Profile Bios and Links

In the world of social media, your profile bio and links serve as the digital handshake that welcomes potential followers to your online persona. An optimized bio is more than just a few lines of text; it is a powerful tool that conveys your identity, purpose, and value. To effectively capture attention, start by clearly articulating who you are and what your AI influencer represents. Use engaging language that resonates with your target audience. Incorporate keywords related to your niche to enhance discoverability and make it easier for users to find you in searches.

Your bio should reflect your unique personality and the essence of your brand. Don't shy away from showcasing your interests, expertise, and the specific value you bring to your audience. A well-crafted bio can evoke curiosity, prompting visitors to explore your content further. Consider adding a touch of creativity or humor to make your profile stand out. Remember, authenticity is key; let your true self shine through your words, as this will help you build a genuine connection with your followers.

Links in your profile are just as critical as your bio. They serve as gateways to your content, products, or any other platforms where your audience can engage with you further. Choose links that lead to your most valuable resources, such as your website, a landing page for your latest project, or an e-commerce store if you're selling products. Make sure to prioritize these links based on what you want your audience to focus on at any given time. Regularly updating your links can keep your profile fresh and encourage repeat visits from followers interested in your latest offerings.

Utilizing link shorteners or link-in-bio tools can enhance your profile's efficiency. These tools allow you to consolidate multiple links into one, creating a clean and organized appearance. They also provide analytics, enabling you to track which links are performing well and adjust your strategy accordingly. This data can be invaluable in understanding your audience's preferences and optimizing your content to better serve their interests, ultimately driving more traffic and engagement.

Lastly, don't underestimate the power of visuals in your profile. A professional profile picture and an eye-catching cover image can complement your bio and links, making your profile more appealing. Invest time in creating a cohesive visual brand that aligns with your message. This consistency across your profile not only enhances your credibility but also makes you more memorable. By optimizing your profile bios and links, you set the stage for your journey as an AI influencer, paving the way for meaningful connections and monetization opportunities on social media.

Building a Consistent Brand Image

Building a consistent brand image is a crucial step in establishing your AI influencer's presence on social media. A strong and recognizable brand image helps you connect with your audience on a deeper level, creating trust and loyalty. To start this journey, define your AI influencer's personality, values, and mission. What message do you want to convey? Consider the emotions you want your audience to feel when they interact with your content. By laying this groundwork, you set the stage for a cohesive and compelling brand that resonates with followers.

Next, visual elements play a significant role in your brand image. Choose a color palette, typography, and design style that reflect your AI influencer's personality. Consistency in these visual elements across all platforms will help your audience easily identify your content. Invest time in creating high-quality graphics, images, and videos that align with your brand's aesthetic. This attention to detail will elevate your influencer's presence and make your content stand out in a crowded social media landscape.

Voice and tone are equally important in building a consistent brand image. Determine the way your AI influencer communicates with the audience. Are they friendly and casual, or more formal and authoritative? Once you establish this voice, maintain it across all posts, captions, and interactions. Consistency in tone ensures that your audience knows what to expect, fostering a sense of familiarity and connection. Engaging with followers in a way that reflects your influencer's personality encourages them to become loyal supporters.

As you develop your brand image, remember the power of storytelling. Share authentic stories and experiences that align with your influencer's mission and values. This approach not only humanizes your AI influencer but also creates a relatable connection with the audience. Use storytelling to highlight challenges, successes, and lessons learned. By doing so, you invite followers into your journey, making them feel like they are part of something meaningful.

Finally, monitor and adapt your brand image as needed. The digital landscape is always evolving, and so are audience preferences. Stay attuned to feedback and insights from your followers. If you notice a shift in engagement or interest, don't hesitate to adjust your brand image while remaining true to your core values. By being responsive to your audience, you reinforce their trust and strengthen your AI influencer's position in the ever-changing world of social media. Embrace this journey, and watch your consistent brand image pave the way to social media success.

Chapter 8: Growing Your Following

Strategies for Gaining Followers

To successfully gain followers for your AI influencer, it is essential to establish a strong and authentic presence across social media platforms. Start by defining your niche clearly, as this will help you attract a specific audience interested in your content. Research trends and topics that resonate with your target demographic, ensuring that your posts are not only engaging but also relevant. Consistency in your messaging and branding will strengthen your identity, making it easier for potential followers to connect with your AI persona.

Another crucial strategy involves leveraging collaborations and partnerships. Engage with other influencers or content creators within your niche to broaden your reach. By collaborating on projects, shout-outs, or joint giveaways, you can tap into their followers and introduce your AI influencer to a wider audience. This mutual benefit fosters a sense of community and can lead to increased credibility and visibility for your brand, ultimately driving follower growth.

Engagement is key in building a loyal follower base. Focus on interacting with your audience by responding to comments, asking questions, and encouraging discussions. Utilize polls, quizzes, and live sessions to make your followers feel involved and valued. The more you engage with them, the more likely they are to share your content with their networks, further amplifying your reach. Remember, genuine interactions can create a devoted community that supports and promotes your AI influencer.

Utilizing data analytics to understand your audience's preferences is another effective strategy. Monitor which types of content garner the most interaction and adjust your strategy accordingly. Use insights to refine your approach, whether it's optimizing posting times, experimenting with different formats, or identifying trending topics. By being data-driven, you can create content that resonates with your followers, encouraging them to stick around and share your posts with others.

Finally, invest in paid promotions to boost your visibility. While organic growth is valuable, sometimes a little extra push can significantly increase your follower count. Use targeted ads to reach specific demographics interested in your niche. Tailor your advertisements to highlight the unique value your AI influencer brings to the table. With a well-crafted promotional strategy, you can accelerate your growth and create a robust following ready to engage with your content and support your journey toward monetization.

Collaborating with Other Influencers

Collaborating with other influencers can significantly amplify your reach and enhance your credibility in the crowded social media landscape. When you partner with individuals who share a similar audience or niche, you not only gain access to their followers but also enrich your content by combining unique perspectives and strengths. Start by identifying influencers whose values align with yours and who are eager to engage in mutually beneficial partnerships. This collaborative spirit can open doors to new opportunities and innovative ideas that can elevate your AI influencer journey.

Once you have identified potential collaborators, reach out with a clear proposal outlining the benefits of the partnership. Be genuine in your approach, expressing your admiration for their work and how you envision the collaboration. Propose specific ideas for joint content, such as live sessions, interviews, or co-created posts, to demonstrate your commitment and creativity. Remember, effective communication is key to building a successful partnership, so be open to their ideas and suggestions as well. This cooperative dialogue sets the stage for a productive relationship that can lead to exciting projects.

As you embark on collaborative projects, ensure that you maintain your unique voice and brand identity. While it's essential to integrate your collaborator's style and ideas, your audience follows you for a specific reason. Strive for a balance that showcases both influencers while keeping the authenticity of your content intact. This approach not only engages your existing followers but also intrigues the new audience you're reaching through your collaborator. The synergy created can lead to a richer experience for everyone involved.

Promoting your collaborative content is crucial for maximizing its impact. Share the joint posts across all your social media platforms, tagging your collaborator to encourage cross-promotion. Utilize engaging captions and compelling visuals to attract attention and drive engagement. Moreover, consider hosting giveaways or contests that involve both your audiences, further increasing visibility and encouraging interaction. The excitement generated from these activities can lead to increased follower counts and greater interest in your individual brands.

Finally, reflect on the outcomes of your collaborations and use these insights to refine your future partnership strategies. Analyze engagement metrics, follower growth, and audience feedback to determine what worked well and what could be improved. This evaluation process will not only help you understand the dynamics of influencer collaborations but also strengthen your approach moving forward. Embrace the journey of collaboration as a powerful tool in your AI influencer toolkit, knowing that each partnership brings you one step closer to achieving social media success and financial growth.

Utilizing Hashtags and Trends

Utilizing hashtags and trends is a powerful strategy that can significantly increase the visibility of your AI influencer on social media. Hashtags serve as a bridge connecting your content with users who share similar interests. By meticulously researching and selecting relevant hashtags, you can ensure that your posts reach a broader audience beyond your immediate followers. Engage with trending hashtags to tap into conversations that are currently capturing attention. This not only helps in gaining visibility but also positions your AI influencer as a relevant voice in ongoing discussions.

To maximize the impact of hashtags, it's essential to strike a balance between popular and niche tags. While trending hashtags can drive a surge of temporary traffic, niche hashtags often attract a more engaged audience that is genuinely interested in your content. Aim to incorporate a mix of both to enhance your reach. Tools like hashtag generators or social media analytics can assist in identifying the most effective hashtags for your posts. Experimenting with different combinations over time can lead to a deeper understanding of what works best for your AI influencer.

Staying on top of current trends is equally vital. Social media is constantly evolving, and being aware of the latest trends can position your AI influencer as a forward-thinking entity. Regularly browsing through trending topics can inspire content ideas that resonate with your audience. You can create posts that either align with these trends or offer a unique perspective on them. This approach not only boosts engagement but also establishes your AI influencer as a thought leader, making it easier to monetize content in the long run.

Engagement is key in social media success, and utilizing hashtags and trends can foster a sense of community around your AI influencer. Encourage your followers to use specific hashtags related to your content, creating a unique space for discussions and interactions. Responding to comments and participating in trending conversations will enhance your presence and make your audience feel valued. When followers see that you actively engage with them, they are more likely to share your content, further amplifying your reach.

In conclusion, the strategic use of hashtags and trends is an essential component of building a successful AI influencer. By combining thoughtful hashtag selection with timely engagement in trends, you can create a dynamic and appealing presence on social media. This not only increases visibility but also cultivates a loyal following, setting the stage for monetization opportunities. Remember, the key is to be authentic and consistent, as these elements will resonate with your audience and help your AI influencer thrive in the digital landscape.

Chapter 9: Monetizing Your AI Influencer

Understanding Different Revenue Streams

Understanding different revenue streams is essential for anyone looking to monetize their AI influencer effectively. As you embark on the journey of creating an AI influencer, it's vital to recognize that income can come from various avenues. By diversifying your revenue streams, you can build a more resilient and profitable online presence. This understanding will empower you to make informed decisions as you navigate the dynamic world of social media.

One of the primary revenue streams to consider is brand partnerships. Companies are constantly on the lookout for innovative ways to reach their target audiences, and having an AI influencer can offer them a unique edge. By showcasing products or services through your AI persona, you can earn money through sponsored posts, affiliate marketing, or even long-term collaborations. Focus on building a strong personal brand and engaging content that aligns with your influencer's niche, as this will attract potential partners eager to leverage your reach.

Another lucrative option is creating and selling digital products. Whether it's eBooks, courses, or exclusive content, your AI influencer can serve as a platform for sharing knowledge and skills with your audience. This approach not only generates income but also positions your influencer as an expert in their field. By identifying the needs and interests of your audience, you can tailor your offerings to ensure they resonate and provide real value, leading to higher sales and customer satisfaction.

Additionally, subscription models have gained popularity as a viable revenue stream. Platforms like Patreon allow creators to offer exclusive content to subscribers in exchange for a monthly fee. This model fosters a sense of community and loyalty among your audience, giving them access to behind-the-scenes insights, special content, or direct interactions with your AI influencer. By consistently delivering high-quality and engaging material, you can build a steady income stream while also strengthening your relationship with followers.

Finally, consider leveraging the power of merchandise. Your AI influencer can become a brand in its own right, allowing you to create and sell products that resonate with your audience. From clothing and accessories to digital art, the possibilities are endless. This not only provides another revenue stream but also enhances your influencer's visibility and reach. As your audience identifies with your AI persona, they will likely want to express that connection through products that reflect the unique identity you have crafted.

By understanding and exploring these diverse revenue streams, you can create a sustainable and profitable business model for your AI influencer. Embrace the opportunities that come with each avenue and remain adaptable as trends evolve. With dedication and creativity, your AI influencer can thrive in the competitive landscape of social media, turning passion into profit.

Affiliate Marketing and Sponsorships

Affiliate marketing and sponsorships are two powerful avenues for monetizing your AI influencer once you've established a presence on social media. By strategically partnering with brands and promoting their products or services, you can generate income while providing value to your audience. This subchapter will guide you through understanding the mechanics of both affiliate marketing and sponsorships, enabling you to leverage these strategies effectively.

To embark on your affiliate marketing journey, start by identifying products or services that resonate with your target audience. Choose affiliates that align with your influencer's niche and values, as authenticity is key. Once you've selected suitable affiliate programs, create engaging content that showcases these products in a relatable manner. This could involve product reviews, tutorials, or even lifestyle posts that seamlessly incorporate the items. By doing so, you not only promote the products but also build trust with your audience, which is crucial for successful conversions.

As your AI influencer gains traction, brands will begin to take notice. Sponsorships are a fantastic way to create a win-win scenario where both you and the brand benefit. To attract sponsorships, it's essential to maintain a consistent and engaging online presence. Showcase your unique voice and style, and focus on growing your follower base. Brands are looking for influencers who can authentically connect with their audience, so ensure your content reflects your personality while also highlighting the potential for brand collaborations.

When negotiating sponsorship deals, be clear about your expectations and the value you bring to the table. Create a media kit that outlines your follower demographics, engagement rates, and previous collaborations. This professional approach will position you as a serious influencer and increase your chances of securing lucrative partnerships. Remember, it's not just about the monetary aspect; a good sponsorship deal should also align with your brand and enhance your credibility within your niche.

Lastly, consistently evaluate the effectiveness of your affiliate marketing and sponsorship efforts. Track metrics such as click-through rates, conversion rates, and audience engagement to understand what resonates best with your followers. This data will not only help you refine your strategies but also make you more appealing to potential sponsors. By remaining adaptable and committed to your audience's needs, you'll carve out a successful path for your AI influencer, turning your passion into a sustainable income stream.

Creating and Selling Products

Creating and selling products as an AI influencer can be an exciting journey that not only enhances your brand but also generates revenue. The first step is to identify a niche that aligns with your personal interests and the needs of your audience. Research trends within your chosen niche to understand what products resonate most with followers. Utilize tools like social media insights and online surveys to gather feedback. This process will help you tailor your products, ensuring they are not only appealing but also valuable to your audience.

Once you have a clear understanding of your niche, the next step is to brainstorm product ideas. These can range from digital downloads such as eBooks and courses to physical merchandise like apparel or tech gadgets. Consider creating exclusive content that showcases your expertise as an AI influencer. For instance, an online course teaching followers how to leverage AI tools for their own social media success can be highly attractive. The key is to provide solutions that solve problems or enhance your audience's experience, making them eager to invest in what you offer.

After developing your product ideas, focus on the creation process. If you're venturing into digital products, make sure to use high-quality tools and software to ensure a polished final product. For physical goods, research reliable suppliers and manufacturers who can align with your brand values. Don't hesitate to seek help from professionals if needed, as quality is paramount. The more effort you put into creating an exceptional product, the more likely it is to stand out in a crowded market.

Marketing your products effectively is crucial for driving sales. Leverage your existing social media platforms to build anticipation before launching. Utilize engaging content, such as sneak peeks or behind-the-scenes looks, to create buzz. Collaborate with other influencers or run targeted ads to expand your reach. Remember, authenticity is key; share your personal journey in creating the product to foster a connection with your audience. Engaging storytelling can significantly enhance interest and motivate followers to support your endeavors.

Finally, maintain a relationship with your customers after the sale. Encourage feedback and actively engage with those who purchase your products. This not only helps you refine future offerings but also builds a loyal community around your brand. Consider implementing loyalty programs or exclusive offers for repeat customers. As your audience sees the value in what you provide, they will become your strongest advocates, helping to grow your influence and income on social media. Embrace this process, and remember that every step you take brings you closer to becoming a successful AI influencer.

Chapter 10: Measuring Success

Key Metrics to Track

When embarking on the journey to create your AI influencer, tracking the right metrics is crucial to ensuring success on social media. The first key metric to consider is engagement rate. This metric measures how actively your audience interacts with your content through likes, comments, shares, and saves. A high engagement rate signifies that your audience finds your content valuable and relatable. By regularly monitoring this metric, you can identify which types of posts resonate most with your followers, allowing you to refine your content strategy and boost your influencer's appeal.

Another essential metric is follower growth rate. This metric not only indicates how quickly your audience is expanding but also reflects the effectiveness of your marketing efforts. A steady growth rate suggests that your AI influencer is gaining traction and attracting interest in your niche. To optimize your growth, engage with your audience consistently, collaborate with other influencers, and use targeted hashtags. Remember, quality often trumps quantity; a smaller, engaged community can be more beneficial than a large, inactive following.

Additionally, tracking reach and impressions will provide insights into how many people are actually seeing your content. While reach measures the total number of unique users who view your posts, impressions count the total number of times your content is displayed, regardless of whether it was clicked or not. Understanding these metrics can help you determine the effectiveness of your promotional strategies and content distribution. If your reach is low, it may indicate that you need to enhance your visibility through better timing, strategic partnerships, or paid promotions.

Conversion rate is another vital metric to track, especially if your goal is to monetize your AI influencer. This metric gauges the percentage of followers who take a desired action, such as clicking a link in your bio or making a purchase through your affiliate links. By analyzing your conversion rates, you can identify which content drives sales and adjust your approach accordingly. Experiment with different calls to action, promotional strategies, and content formats to see what leads to higher conversions, ensuring that your AI influencer becomes a profitable venture.

Finally, don't overlook the importance of sentiment analysis. By assessing the tone of comments and interactions surrounding your content, you can gauge how your audience feels about your brand. Positive sentiment can lead to increased loyalty and word-of-mouth promotion, while negative sentiment may require adjustments in your approach. Tools and analytics platforms can help you track sentiment over time, enabling you to make informed decisions that align with your audience's preferences and foster a thriving online community. Embracing these key metrics will empower you to build a successful AI influencer and achieve your social media goals.

Analyzing Engagement and Reach

Engagement and reach are two critical metrics that define the success of your AI influencer on social media. Understanding these concepts is essential for crafting a strategy that maximizes your impact and profitability. Engagement refers to the level of interaction your content receives from your audience, including likes, comments, shares, and saves. Reach, on the other hand, indicates the total number of unique users who have seen your content. By analyzing these metrics, you can refine your approach, ensuring that your AI influencer resonates with the target audience and drives meaningful conversations.

To analyze engagement, start by monitoring key performance indicators (KPIs) such as engagement rate, which is calculated by dividing the total interactions by the number of followers. A high engagement rate suggests that your audience finds your content valuable and is likely to share it with others. Don't shy away from experimenting with different types of content—videos, polls, and stories can evoke varied responses. By actively responding to comments and fostering a community around your AI influencer, you can enhance engagement, making followers feel heard and valued.

Next, consider reach as a pivotal element in expanding your AI influencer's audience. Tools like social media analytics can provide insights into how far your posts travel across platforms. Pay attention to the times and days when your content garners the most visibility. This information can guide your posting schedule, enabling you to reach more users when they are most active. Collaborating with other influencers or brands can also amplify your reach, introducing your AI influencer to new audiences and creating opportunities for monetization.

As you delve into analyzing engagement and reach, it's vital to remain adaptable. Trends in social media can shift rapidly, so staying informed about what resonates with your audience is crucial. Regularly reviewing your analytics will help you identify patterns and preferences, allowing you to refine your content strategy. Embrace feedback and use it to pivot when necessary. A proactive approach will not only improve your influencer's performance but will also solidify your reputation as a savvy social media strategist.

Lastly, remember that both engagement and reach are interconnected. A strategy that fosters genuine interaction will naturally lead to increased reach over time. As your AI influencer builds a loyal following, word-of-mouth recommendations will boost visibility, creating a cycle of growth. Stay focused on delivering value, whether through informative content, entertainment, or inspiration. With persistence and a keen eye on your analytics, you can cultivate a thriving AI influencer that not only engages your audience but also generates income through strategic partnerships, sponsorships, and product promotions.

Adjusting Your Strategy Based on Data

In the dynamic realm of social media, data is your most powerful ally. As you embark on the journey of building your AI influencer, understanding and leveraging data can dramatically enhance your strategy. By continuously analyzing performance metrics, audience engagement, and market trends, you can make informed decisions that refine your approach and drive better results. Embrace a mindset of curiosity; the insights you gather will not only inform your content but also empower you to connect more authentically with your audience.

Start by identifying key performance indicators (KPIs) relevant to your AI influencer. These could include engagement rates, follower growth, click-through rates, and conversion metrics. Regularly monitoring these KPIs will provide a clear picture of what resonates with your audience. For instance, if you notice that posts featuring certain themes or formats consistently outperform others, consider increasing your focus on those areas. This iterative process of testing and learning will guide you in fine-tuning your content strategy, ensuring that you remain relevant and engaging.

In addition to tracking your metrics, dive deep into audience analytics. Understanding your audience's demographics, preferences, and online behavior can unlock new opportunities for content creation. Utilize tools that provide insights into who is engaging with your posts and at what times. Tailoring your content to meet the interests of your audience not only boosts engagement but also fosters a sense of community around your AI influencer. Remember, the more you know about your audience, the better equipped you are to create content that speaks directly to them.

Trends in social media are ever-evolving, and staying ahead of the curve is crucial. Regularly analyze broader market trends and emerging technologies within the AI space. This knowledge can help you pivot your strategy when necessary, ensuring that your influencer remains relevant. By being proactive, you can capitalize on new trends before they become mainstream, positioning your AI influencer as a thought leader in your niche. This foresight will not only attract a larger audience but can also open up monetization opportunities through partnerships and collaborations.

Finally, don't hesitate to iterate on your strategy based on the data you collect. The beauty of working in a digital environment is the ability to adapt quickly. If a particular campaign or content piece isn't performing as expected, use that feedback to adjust your approach. Whether it's experimenting with new formats, refining your messaging, or even changing your posting schedule, the flexibility to adapt is what will set you apart. Embrace the journey of growth and learning, and remember that every adjustment you make is a step toward building a successful AI influencer that not only engages but also generates revenue on social media.

Chapter 11: Navigating Challenges

Common Pitfalls to Avoid

Creating an AI influencer can be an exciting journey, but there are common pitfalls that can hinder your success if you're not careful. One of the most significant mistakes is neglecting audience research. Understanding your target audience is crucial for developing content that resonates with them. Failing to identify their preferences, interests, and pain points can lead to a disconnect, making it harder for your AI influencer to gain traction. Take the time to conduct thorough research and create audience personas that will guide your content strategy.

Another common pitfall is underestimating the importance of authenticity. Even though your influencer is AI-generated, the content should still feel genuine and relatable. Audiences can easily spot inauthenticity, which can damage trust and engagement. Strive to create a personality for your AI that reflects real human emotions and values. This connection will foster loyalty and make followers more likely to engage with your content, ultimately driving your success.

Consistency is key when building an AI influencer, yet many creators falter in this area. Inconsistent posting schedules can confuse followers and diminish interest. It's essential to establish a content calendar and stick to it. This not only helps to keep your audience engaged, but it also allows your AI to evolve and adapt its content over time, responding to trends and audience feedback. Regularity breeds familiarity, and that is vital for growing your follower base.

Another pitfall is neglecting the power of collaboration. While you may be focused on developing your own AI influencer, collaborating with other influencers or brands can create valuable opportunities for exposure and growth. Partnering with others can introduce your AI to new audiences and provide fresh content ideas that keep your followers engaged. Don't hesitate to reach out to others in your niche; mutual support can be incredibly beneficial.

Finally, overlooking analytics can severely impact your progress. Many creators create content without measuring its effectiveness. Regularly reviewing your analytics is essential for understanding what works and what doesn't. Use the insights gained from your data to refine your strategy, improve content quality, and make informed decisions about your AI influencer's direction. By avoiding these common pitfalls and staying committed to your vision, you can successfully build a thriving AI influencer that captivates and monetizes your audience.

Handling Negative Feedback

Handling negative feedback is an inevitable part of building your AI influencer brand on social media. While it can feel disheartening to receive criticism, viewing it as an opportunity for growth can transform your approach and enhance your influence. Negative feedback often highlights areas where your content or strategy may need adjustment. By embracing this feedback with an open mind, you can fine-tune your messaging and better resonate with your audience, ultimately strengthening your brand.

When faced with negative comments or reviews, it's crucial to remain calm and composed. Take a moment to process your emotions before responding. This pause allows you to approach the situation with a level head, which is essential for addressing concerns effectively. A thoughtful response can demonstrate your commitment to your audience and willingness to improve. This not only helps in resolving the situation but also showcases your professionalism—a trait that can attract even more followers who appreciate your approach.

Engaging with your audience is vital when handling criticism. Rather than ignoring negative feedback, acknowledge it and show gratitude for the input. This openness can create a more positive dialogue and encourage your followers to share their thoughts without fear of backlash. By fostering a culture of communication, you not only address the specific concern but also cultivate a loyal community that feels valued and heard. Remember, your audience is more likely to stick around if they see you actively working to improve based on their feedback.

Leveraging negative feedback for content creation is another effective strategy. Use the insights gained from criticism to create informative and engaging posts that address the concerns raised. For example, if a common complaint revolves around the clarity of your AI influencer's messaging, consider crafting a tutorial or a Q&A session that clarifies your points. This proactive approach not only addresses the feedback but also showcases your ability to adapt and evolve, reinforcing your credibility in the social media landscape.

Finally, it's important to maintain a positive mindset throughout this process. Negative feedback is often more reflective of the reviewer's personal experience than an absolute judgment of your work. By focusing on the constructive aspects and recognizing that not every comment will resonate with you, you can build resilience. This resilience is key to your long-term success as an AI influencer. Embrace the journey, learn from the feedback, and continue to innovate; your ability to navigate challenges will ultimately set you apart in the competitive world of social media.

Staying Ahead of Trends

Staying ahead of trends is crucial in the fast-paced world of social media, especially for those looking to build an AI influencer. To successfully navigate this landscape, it is essential to remain vigilant and proactive in identifying emerging trends that resonate with your target audience. By tapping into current conversations and cultural shifts, you can position your AI influencer as a relevant and influential voice within your niche. This proactive approach not only enhances your influencer's visibility but also fosters a deeper connection with followers who seek authenticity and innovation.

One effective strategy for staying ahead of trends is to actively engage with various social media platforms and their communities. Regularly explore trending hashtags, popular content formats, and emerging challenges to gain insights into what captures the audience's attention. Consider leveraging tools like Google Trends, BuzzSumo, or social listening platforms that analyze data across social media networks. By understanding what content is resonating with users, you can tailor your AI influencer's messaging and visuals to align with those trends, ensuring that your content remains fresh and appealing.

Collaboration is another powerful way to keep your AI influencer at the forefront of trends. Partnering with other creators, brands, or influencers can help you access new audiences and incorporate different perspectives into your content. Look for opportunities to co-create content that highlights trending topics, challenges, or popular themes. These collaborations can not only enhance your influencer's credibility but also spark innovative ideas that push the envelope of creativity, ensuring your content stands out in a crowded marketplace.

Continual learning is vital in this ever-evolving digital landscape. Stay informed about the latest developments in technology, social media algorithms, and user preferences. Attend webinars, follow industry leaders, and read relevant articles to keep your knowledge up to date. Make it a habit to analyze the performance of your content regularly. By understanding what works and what doesn't, you can pivot your strategy to embrace new trends and ideas that will keep your AI influencer relevant and engaging.

Finally, don't be afraid to experiment and take risks. The social media landscape thrives on creativity and innovation, and your willingness to try new things will set your AI influencer apart. Whether it's adopting a new content format, exploring unconventional themes, or utilizing cutting-edge technology, being open to experimentation can lead to exciting opportunities. Embrace the journey of staying ahead of trends, and you will not only build a successful AI influencer but also create a brand that resonates deeply with your audience and generates income in the process.

Chapter 12: Future of AI Influencers

Emerging Technologies

Emerging technologies are revolutionizing the way we create and engage with AI influencers, providing exciting opportunities for those looking to carve a niche in the social media landscape. As these technologies continue to evolve, they offer innovative tools that empower creators to design more authentic and engaging personas. By harnessing advancements in artificial intelligence, machine learning, and augmented reality, aspiring influencers can not only enhance their content but also connect with their audiences on a deeper level. Embracing these technologies is not just about staying current; it's about positioning yourself at the forefront of the digital revolution.

One of the most significant advancements in AI is the development of sophisticated natural language processing tools. These tools enable AI influencers to engage in human-like conversations, responding to comments and messages in real-time while maintaining a consistent brand voice. This level of interactivity can help foster a loyal community, as followers feel valued and heard. By utilizing these technologies, you can create a more personalized experience for your audience, which not only enhances engagement but also increases the likelihood of monetization through sponsorships and partnerships.

Visual content is another area where emerging technologies are making waves. Tools powered by deep learning can analyze trending visual styles and recommend creative elements that resonate with your target audience. From generating eye-catching graphics to crafting compelling video content, these technologies can streamline your creative process and help you produce high-quality materials more efficiently. By leveraging these tools, you can stand out in a crowded marketplace and attract potential sponsors who are eager to collaborate with fresh and innovative influencers.

Augmented reality (AR) is also transforming the influencer landscape, offering unique ways to engage audiences. With AR, you can create interactive experiences that captivate followers and encourage them to share your content. Imagine launching a campaign where users can virtually try on products or participate in immersive challenges. Such engaging experiences not only bolster your brand's presence but also open up new avenues for monetization through collaborations with brands seeking to tap into the excitement of AR technology. By embracing these innovative approaches, you position yourself as a trendsetter within your niche.

As you explore these emerging technologies, remember that the key to success lies in authenticity. While it's tempting to rely solely on cutting-edge tools, it's essential to maintain a genuine connection with your audience. Use these technologies as an enhancement rather than a replacement for your unique voice and personality. By striking the right balance, you can build a compelling AI influencer that resonates with your followers, turning passion into profit. Embrace the future of social media with confidence, and watch as your AI influencer journey unfolds into a thriving venture.

The Evolving Landscape of Social Media

The landscape of social media is constantly evolving, presenting both challenges and opportunities for those looking to create an AI influencer. As platforms innovate and adapt to user behavior, understanding these shifts is crucial for anyone aiming to make their mark in this dynamic environment. What was once dominated by personal influencers has now opened up a space for AI-driven personalities, enabling creators to harness technology and creativity in ways previously unimaginable. This evolution empowers you to explore uncharted territories and connect with audiences on a deeper level.

As social media platforms refine their algorithms, it becomes increasingly important to stay ahead of trends. By leveraging AI, you can analyze vast amounts of data to determine what content resonates with your target audience. This analytical approach not only enhances your ability to craft engaging posts but also allows you to identify the best times to share your content for maximum visibility. Embracing these tools can significantly boost your chances of success, making your AI influencer stand out in a crowded marketplace.

The rise of video content, particularly short-form videos, has transformed how audiences engage with influencers. Platforms like TikTok and Instagram Reels have shifted the focus towards creativity and authenticity, encouraging influencers to tell stories in engaging, bite-sized formats. This trend opens the door for AI influencers to use innovative storytelling techniques that captivate viewers. By experimenting with different video styles and formats, you can create compelling narratives that not only entertain but also drive monetization opportunities through brand partnerships and sponsorships.

Moreover, the increasing importance of community building cannot be overlooked. As social media becomes more crowded, audiences seek genuine connections and shared values. AI influencers have the unique ability to interact with followers in real-time, using data-driven insights to tailor their engagement strategies. By fostering a sense of community, you can cultivate loyal followings that not only support your content but are also eager to promote your brand. This loyal base is essential for driving revenue streams, whether through merchandise sales, affiliate marketing, or exclusive content offerings.

Finally, as the regulatory landscape around social media continues to shift, staying informed about best practices and ethical considerations is essential. Transparency and authenticity are becoming paramount, and AI influencers must navigate these waters thoughtfully. By adhering to guidelines and prioritizing ethical engagement, you can build a reputable brand that resonates with your audience. The evolving landscape offers you a unique opportunity to not just create an AI influencer but to establish a meaningful presence that can thrive and generate income in the ever-changing world of social media.

Preparing for the Next Wave of Change

As we navigate the ever-evolving landscape of social media, it's crucial to prepare for the next wave of change that will undoubtedly impact how AI influencers operate. The rise of artificial intelligence has already transformed content creation, audience engagement, and brand partnerships. To stay ahead, you must embrace this transformation and equip yourself with the knowledge and tools necessary to thrive. Understanding emerging trends, such as personalization and augmented reality, will allow you to position your AI influencer for success and create content that resonates with your audience.

Investing time in continuous learning is essential for anyone looking to create an AI influencer. Stay updated on the latest advancements in AI technology, social media algorithms, and user preferences. This could mean following industry leaders, participating in webinars, or engaging with online communities focused on AI and influencer marketing. By keeping your fingers on the pulse of these developments, you will gain insights that can guide your strategy and help you adapt your approach as new opportunities arise.

Collaborating with experts in various fields can also enhance your preparation for upcoming changes. Seek out partnerships with data scientists, digital marketers, and social media strategists who can provide valuable perspectives and advice. These collaborations can help you refine your content strategy, optimize your AI algorithms, and ensure that your influencer remains relevant in a rapidly changing environment. Surrounding yourself with knowledgeable individuals will not only expand your skill set but also foster creativity and innovation in your approach.

Building a flexible and adaptive brand identity is another crucial aspect of preparing for future changes. Your AI influencer should be able to pivot and evolve in response to shifting trends, audience preferences, and technological advancements. This means developing a brand that reflects not only your current vision but is also open to transformation. Regularly assess your content and engagement strategies, and be willing to experiment with new formats and platforms. This adaptability will ensure that your influencer remains fresh and appealing to your audience.

Finally, embrace a mindset of resilience and positivity as you prepare for the next wave of change. The journey to create a successful AI influencer can be challenging, filled with ups and downs. However, viewing these challenges as opportunities for growth will empower you to navigate obstacles with confidence. By maintaining a forward-looking perspective and being proactive about your preparation, you can lay a solid foundation for your AI influencer's success and ultimately turn your passion into profit on social media.